HORRIBLE HISTORIES

ANNUAL 2014

TERRY DEARY ✳ **MARTIN BROWN**

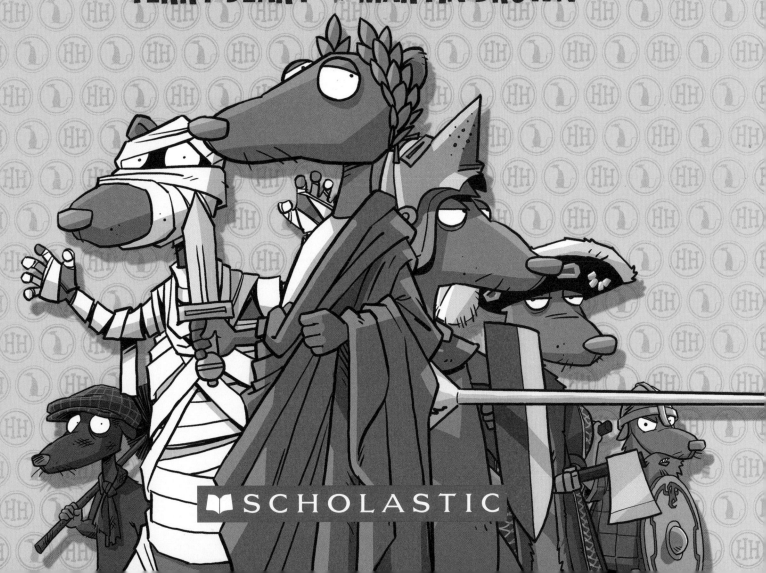

SCHOLASTIC

CONTENTS

This **Horrible Annual** belongs to:

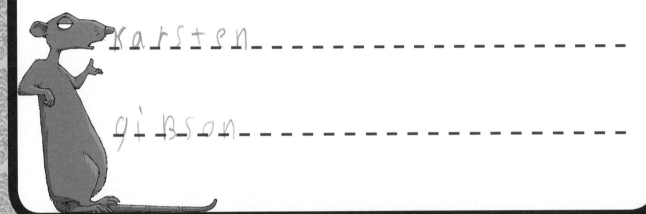

karsten

gibson

ALL ABOUT HORRIBLE YOU

I get asked a lot of questions about "history" when I meet my readers. Now it's time to turn the tables and ask YOU those questions ... tell the truth or suffer the terrible Horrible Histories torture of being nibbled to death by ducks. Ready?

What is your favourite period in history?

Why do you like that period?

Who is your favourite character in history?

----

and why?

If you could bring anyone back to life who would you rather NOT meet from history?

- 8

hitler and king henry 8 th

If you could have a new Horrible Histories book then what would it be about?

and what would you call it?

HORRIBLE HISTORIES

draw your cover here

TERRY DEARY

AWFUL EGYPTIAN GRISLY GALLERY

NARMER (ruled around 3150 BC)
How did he get to be pharaoh? By being super- cruel. Pictures show him holding a prisoner on the end of a rope ... and the  rope has been pushed through a hole in the prisoner's nose. Ouch. Who knows how got his power? There are also pictures of his enemies lying on the ground – have they just nodded off? No, because they're headless – sort of noddle off.

 **DJOSER** (ruled 2668–2649 BC)
He built the first of the great pyramids then he died and was made into a mummy. His insides were packed into containers called canopic jars – one each for his liver, his stomach, his guts and his lungs. But he was king of South Egypt and North Egypt. To keep the people in both parts of the country happy he had to be buried in two different tombs. His body was entombed in the north, and his canopic jars had their own temple 100 metres to the south.

KHUFU (ruled 2589–2566 BC)
This pharaoh has the biggest pyramid, the biggest statue and the biggest ships in Egypt. After his death his son  had two ships buried beside his great pyramid at Giza. The ships were found in 30-metre pits. The ships were taken apart before they were buried. What was found was a sort of ship kit pit. The spirit of the ship would carry the spirit of the pharaoh to the afterlife.

 **PEPI II** (ruled 2278–2184 or 2218 BC)
No one can agree how long this pharaoh ruled, but most agree that he came to the throne when he was only six years old.

He wasn't interested in war or pyramids. He was only interested in getting a dwarf for his palace. His army set off into Africa and reports came back that they had captured a pygmy. He wrote a message to his general telling him how to treat the captured pygmy. The pygmy got to the palace safely.

TAO I (ruled around 1560 BC)

Around 1650 BC the Hyksos people from Asia invaded Egypt and took over the north. The Egyptians went on ruling in the south.

This pharaoh and his Egyptians rose up against the Hyksos. His mummy was discovered at Deir el-Bahari in 1881. The skull showed terrible wounds, but not the sort he would have got if he had been standing up and fighting – he was lying on his right side. Was he knocked down and hacked? Or was he murdered in his sleep?

HATSHEPSUT (ruled 1479-1457 BC)

This pharaoh was a bit odd because she was actually a she – one of the few ancient Egyptian woman pharaohs. Pharaoh Tuthmosis II was supposed to rule, but he was only a child when his father died, so his bossy step-mother helped him. In the end she also helped herself – to the throne and called herself pharaoh and did all the things that pharaohs did... Of course it couldn't last. She died... And Tuthmosis may have had something to do with it.

TUTHMOSIS III (ruled 1479-1425 BC)

This pharaoh officially came to the throne in 1479 BC, but he spent 22 years being ruled by his step-mother. So when he got the throne he tried to prove that he wasn't really such a wimp. He had stories carved in temples that said things like I have killed seven lions and 12 wild bulls all by myself. But it took him 20 years to kill one step- mother.

RAMESSES II – THE GREAT
(ruled 1279-1212 BC)

This pharaoh made the Hebrews his slaves. The Bible tells their story. Their leader begged the pharaoh to set them free but he wouldn't budge. So God made the rivers run with blood and in each Egyptian family, the oldest child died in the night.

The pharaoh changed his mind. The Hebrews headed home. But the pharaoh sent an army after them. So God made a path through the sea for the Hebrew slaves. When the Egyptian army tried to follow, God let the waters rush back and they were all drowned.

AMENHOTEP IV (ruled about 1353-1336 BC)

Egyptian kings liked to think they died and joined the other gods in heaven. This pharaoh couldn't wait. He said he was a god on Earth. He wrecked the temples and statues of other gods saying, "There's just one god. The sun god. And that's me, folks!" The priests of Amun were upset and may have smashed up his mummy to stop him from getting to heaven. His mummy has never been found...

CLEOPATRA (ruled from 51-30 BC)

This pharaoh shared the throne with her little brother Ptolemy XIII. After she met top Roman ruler Julius Caesar she didn't need little brother – and little brother was discovered drowned. She married her other little brother, Ptolemy XIV, and guess what? Ptolemy was murdered. Caesar came to a sticky end, so she moved on to Roman general Mark Antony, but they lost a war against Rome. The famous story is she killed herself, bitten by a poisonous snake ... an asp.

GROOVY GREEK GAMES

Greek children invented games like knucklebones that are still played in some parts of the world today. In fact you may even have played some of the games yourself. If you haven't, and want to play like a groovy Greek, then here are the rules for six games.

OSTRAKINDA

This is a game for two teams that is still played in Italy, Germany and France.

You need: A silver coin. Paint one side black with poster paint - this side is 'Night'. The plain side is 'Day'.

Rules:

1 Divide into two teams – the 'Nights' and the 'Days'.

2 Spin the coin in the air.

3 If it lands black side up then the Nights chase the Days – and if it lands silver side up the Days chase the Nights.

COOKING POT

Rules:

1 Choose someone to be 'It'.

2 'It' is blindfolded and sits on the ground.

3 The others try to touch or poke 'It'.

4 'It' aims to touch one of the teasers with a foot.

5 Anyone touched by a foot becomes 'It', is blindfolded and sits on the ground.

BRONZE FLY

A sort of Greek Blind-man's Buff. A Greek described it...

They fastened a head-band round a boy's eyes. He was then turned round and round and called out, "I will chase the bronze fly!"

The others called back, "You might chase him but you won't catch him."

They then torment him with paper whips until he catches one of them.

EPHEDRISMOS

Rules:

1 A player is blindfolded and gives a second one a piggy-back.

2 The rider then has to guide the player to a target set on the ground.

3 If the player succeeds then he becomes the rider. This could become a competition where pairs race to reach the target.

GREECKET

The Greeks also played ball games where you throw a ball at a 'wicket', rather like cricket without a batsman. We just have pictures of these games that have been painted on Greek vases, but we don't have their written rules. Make up your own rules – maybe they played like this...

1 Stand on a mark a fixed distance from the wicket.

2 Take the ball and have ten attempts to hit the wicket.

3 The opponent stands behind the wicket (like a wicket-keeper) and throws the ball back to you every time.

4 Then you stand behind the wicket while your opponent has ten tries.

5 The one who has the most hits of the wicket from ten throws is the winner.

6 Try again from a different mark.

It looks (from the vase paintings) as if the loser has to give the winner a piggy-back ride.

KOTTABOS

Rules:

1 Take a wooden pole and stand it upright.

2 Balance a small metal disk on top of the pole.

3 Leave a little wine in the bottom of your two-handled drinking cup.

4 Grip the cup by one handle, flick the wine out and try to knock the disk off the top of the pole.

(Would you believe grown-up Greeks played this silly game at parties?) You can try this with a cup and water and a 50p coin on the end of a broom handle ... but not in your dining room, please.

Text taken from *Groovy Greeks*.

POMPEII
24 AUGUST AD 79

THE ROMAN EMPERORS WERE MIGHTY MEN WHO STARTED TO TAKE OVER THE WORLD AND TURN IT INTO THE MASSIVE ROMAN EMPIRE. THEY TOOK OVER CITIES. BUT SOMETIMES THEY LIVED - AND DIED - TO REGRET IT. TAKE THE CITY OF POMPEII, FOR EXAMPLE...

HIGH-SPEED HISTORY

THE ROMANS CAME TO POMPE...

WELCOME TO THE CITY OF POMPEII ... SIR

SHOW US AROUND YOUR CONQUERED CITY, MY MAN!

YOU DON'T REALLY WANT TO LIVE HERE, IT'S AN UNLUCKY PLACE!

NONSENSE!

THERE WERE SMALLER EARTHQUAKES. POMPEII WASN'T RUINED BY THEM ... BUT THEY STIRRED UP THE MIGHTY VOLCANO THAT STOOD JUST SIX MILES DOWN THE ROAD ... VESUVIUS. IT BEGAN TO SMOKE A LITTLE...

THE NEW POMPEII WAS ALMOST FINISHED BY THE AUTUMN OF AD 79.

WELCOME BACK, SIR. POMPEII IS NOW AS FINE AS ROME.

WE HAVE FOUR PUBLIC BATHS

ROME HAS MORE

IT'S THE GOD OF FIRE, VULCAN. HE'S ANGRY! WE'RE DOOMED

YES, I ALWAYS SAID SMOKING IS BAD FOR US

WE GET THOUSANDS OF PEOPLE BATHING IN THEM EVERY WEEK

AH! BUT YOU ONLY CHANGE THE WATER ON A MONDAY MORNING!

Over the years much more of Pompeii has been uncovered. Two million people visit it every year. What a cheerful holiday that must be! Go there and see that carving on the floor ... Salve, lucru – 'welcome to money'.

It should have said 'welcome to death'.

FOUL FEASTING

Throughout history there have been some people who ate far more than anyone else. Far more than they needed to eat. Far more than an average person could eat. These sad people are known as gluttons.

In ancient history gluttony was 'good' – it showed the world how wealthy you were. Feasts were a way of showing off – the way rich people these days buy flashy cars. (BMWs hadn't been invented in ancient times.)

Kings, like Henry VIII of England and Louis XIV of France, were famous for their huge meals. But there were foul feasters more than a thousand years before those kings. Here are a few tasty samples...

CALIGULA (ROMAN EMPEROR)

Said to have enjoyed drinking pearls dissolved in vinegar and to have served his guests with loaves and meats made out of gold. To entertain his guests, Caligula had criminals beheaded in the dining room as they feasted. (And some people still like a nice chop for dinner.)

VITELLIUS (ROMAN EMPEROR)

Known as 'The Glutton'. Said to have enjoyed three or four banquets a day. At one, his brother served up 2,000 fish and 7,000 birds. Fave recipe: pike livers, pheasant brains, peacock brains, flamingo tongues and the spleen of eels.

His priests gave sacred cake to the gods. Vitellius couldn't resist pinching it for himself.

NERO (ROMAN EMPEROR)

Nero hired a 'glutton' – a huge Egyptian slave who ate everything he was fed. This was feast-time fun for Nero's guests. What Nero enjoyed most was watching his glutton kill a man and eat him.

ELAGABALUS (ROMAN EMPEROR)

Said to have once served a meal comprising the brains of 600 thrushes. Ate camels' heels and cockerels' crests, flamingo brains, parrots' heads, peacocks' tongues and ostrich brains. He ate roast pig, from which live thrushes flew, and enjoyed African snails. Elagabalus rewarded his cooks for the invention of a new sauce ... unless he didn't like it, in which case he forced them to eat nothing else but that sauce until they came up with one he did like.

ROMAN PRIESTS

Around 70 BC the priests were the biggest eaters in Rome. One of their tastiest treats was pig's udder. The priests also liked eating one food made to look like another. So the cooks made a 'fish' out of a pig's womb, a 'pigeon' out of bacon or a 'dove' out of ham.

NAME THAT NORSEMAN

The people of the 11th century were often named after their appearance. These nicknames were usually invented long after the person died by medieval writers. (It probably would have been a bad idea to go up to a Viking and call him 'Mr Flatnose'.)

Can you spot the real names here?

1 Viking Chief, Thorkell the ...
a) Tall
b) Thin
c) Thick-as-Two-Short Planks

2 Danish conqueror, Svein ...
a) Fork-tongue
b) Forkbeard
c) Fork-and-Knife

3 Ethelred's son, Edmund ...
a) Ironheart
b) Ironside
c) Iron-Me-Shirt

4 Strathclyde king, Owen the ...
a) Bald
b) Hairy
c) Permed

5 Earl of Orkney, Sigurd the ...
a) Stout
b) Slim
c) Stuffed

6 Archbishop of York, Wulfstan the ...
a) Wolf
b) Fox
c) Yeti

7 Duke of Normandy, Robert the ...
a) Saint
b) Devil
c) Slightly Naughty

SOMEHOW I THOUGHT CAMELOT WOULD BE BIGGER

8 King Knut's son, Harold ...
a) Flatfoot
b) Harefoot
c) Five-Foot-Two

9 Norse king of the Irish, Sigtrygg ...
a) Silkbeard
b) Squarebeard
c) Bottle o' Beard

10 Wife of King Harold, Edith ...
a) Swantail
b) Swan-Neck
c) Swansbum

11 King of Norway, Magnus ...
a) Barefoot
b) Bareback
c) Bear-Hug

If you were a Viking what do you think your Norse name would be?

My Norse name would be _Big Leg willy_

the _1 Th_

What would your best friends' Norse names be?

big head chid

What about your pets' Norse names?

billy The willy

Text taken from *Vicious Vikings*.

OK ERIC, YOU'RE THE GREAT NAVIGATOR – WHERE'S THIS BLINKIN' MONASTERY THEN?

OUT OF TIME!

This is London in 1299, but some things are out of place – or rather out of time. Can you work out which things are right and which are wrong?

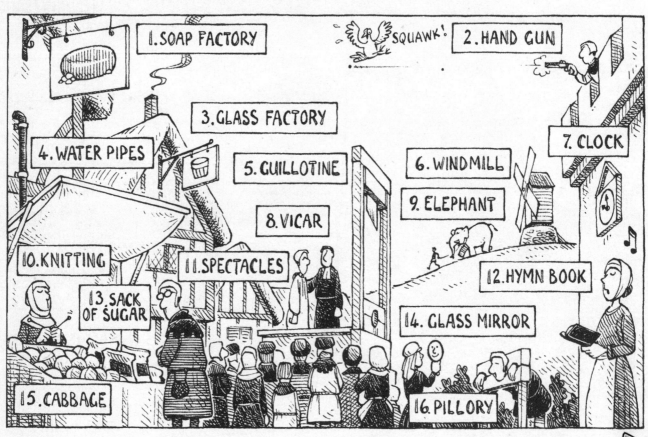

ODD ONE OUT	RIGHT	WRONG		RIGHT	WRONG
1. Soap factory	☐	☐	9. Elephant	☐	☐
2. Hand gun	☐	☐	10. Knitting	☐	☐
3. Glass factory	☐	☐	11. Spectacles	☐	☐
4. Water pipes	☐	☐	12. Hymn book	☐	☐
5. Guillotine	☐	☐	13. Sack of sugar	☐	☐
6. Windmill	☐	☐	14. Glass mirror	☐	☐
7. Clock	☐	☐	15. Cabbage	☐	☐
8. Vicar	☐	☐	16. Pillory	☐	☐

Answers on page 60.

22

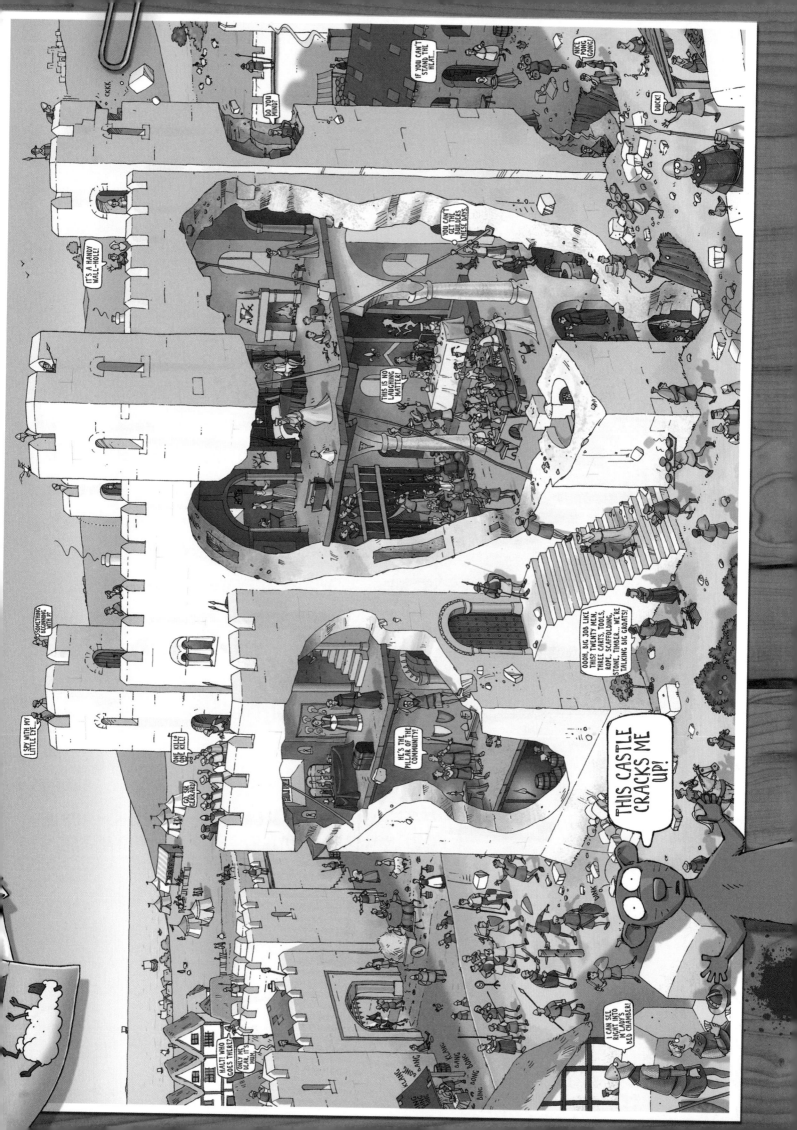

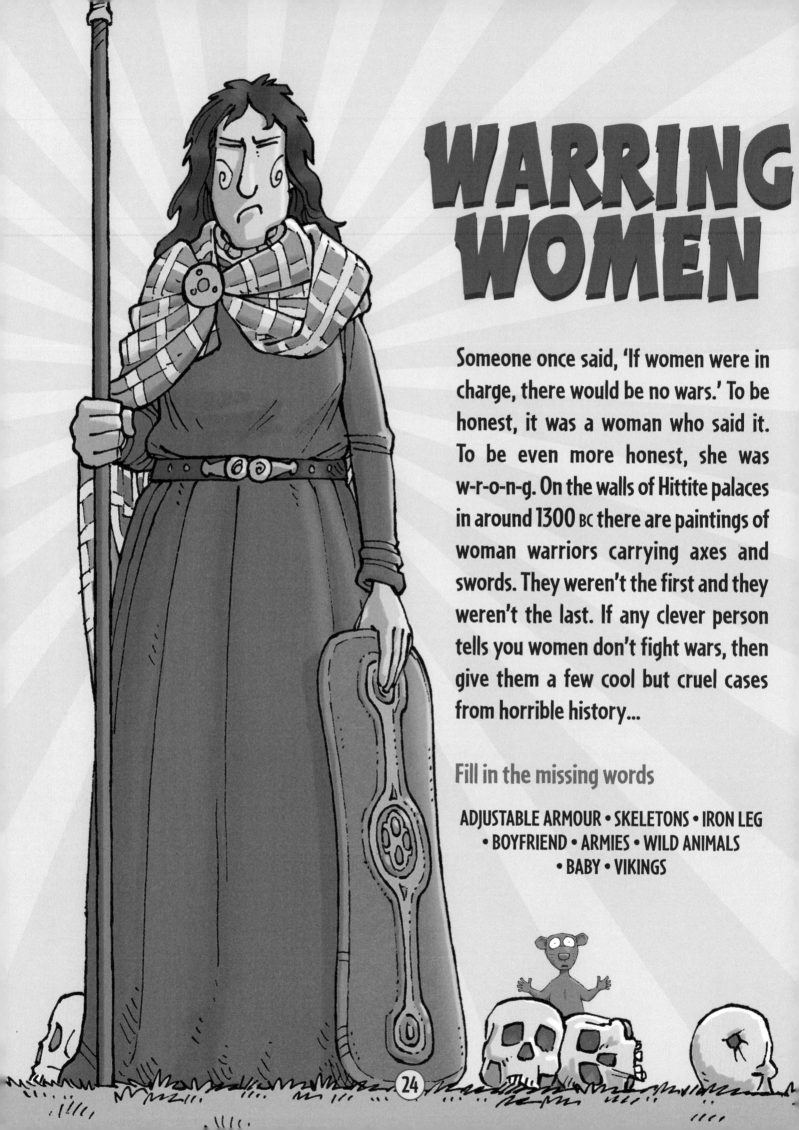

WARRING WOMEN

Someone once said, 'If women were in charge, there would be no wars.' To be honest, it was a woman who said it. To be even more honest, she was w-r-o-n-g. On the walls of Hittite palaces in around 1300 BC there are paintings of woman warriors carrying axes and swords. They weren't the first and they weren't the last. If any clever person tells you women don't fight wars, then give them a few cool but cruel cases from horrible history...

Fill in the missing words

ADJUSTABLE ARMOUR • SKELETONS • IRON LEG
• BOYFRIEND • ARMIES • WILD ANIMALS
• BABY • VIKINGS

The Rig Veda is an ancient sacred poem of India, written between 3500 and 1800 BC. It tells the story of warrior-queen Vishpla, who lost her leg in battle, was fitted with an a)_____ and returned to battle. Iron lady.

The Hebrew wise-woman, Deborah, was a war leader during the occupation of Canaan, 1250–1050 BC. With her advice the Hebrews smashed the b) _____ of Canaan. Bet no one dared to call her Debbie.

The Greeks had legends of a group of women warriors called the Amazons. Some historians think these legends were based on Scythian women of the fourth and fifth centuries BC. Archaeologists have found female c) _____ with bows, swords, and horses.

In AD 39 Trung Trac and Trung Nhi led a Vietnamese revolt against the Chinese. They captured 65 forts and reigned as queens until AD 43. Their mother Tran Thi Doan (also known as Lady Man Thien) trained them in military skills and led troops to support them. Phung Thi Chinh also took part in the Vietnam battles of AD 43 and had her d)_____ at the battlefront. The mother of all battlers.

In AD 366 Empress Jingo Kogo led a Japanese invasion of Korea. She was pregnant at the time and therefore had to have e) _____ made.

In AD 63 Celtic and Roman gladiator shows included 'women of high class'. There was also a female chariot fighter rider who fought against men. In AD 88 women gladiators were described as members of the venatores (gladiators who fought f) _____ in the Roman arena). Emperor Alexander Severus passed a law banning women fighters in the arena in AD 200.

Legendary Celtic women warriors included Medb (Maeve) of Ireland, Aife (Aoife) of Alba (Scotland), and Queen Scathach of Skye. The Romans in Britain fought against Queen Boudica (or Bodiecia, Boadicea, Voadica, Voada) of the Iceni in AD 61. The Romans were allies to Queen Cartimandua of the Brigantes in a war against her g)_____ in AD 43.

In the 900s Queen Thyre of Denmark led her army against the Germans, and in 722 Queen Aethelburgh destroyed Taunton. Also in the 900s Aethelflaed, Lady of Mercia, led troops against the h) _____ and Olga of Russia ended a revolt in which her husband had died.

Answers on page 61.

Text taken from *The Mad Miscellany*.

PLAGUE SONG

The plague starts with a little flea that jumps upon a rat,
It bites the rat and gives it plague germs, for the rat that's that.
Then the flea it looks for somewhere else to find food,
So it hops on you and me and starts to suck our blood.

CHORUS
First you feel a little poorly, then you start to swell
Then you start to spit some blood, and then you really smell
Then you know it's time to ring your fu-ne-ral bell
Then along comes Mister Death and swishes you to ... well!

There's lots of cures to help you if you have the cash,
Kill the village cats and dogs then burn them all to ash.
Sit down in a sewer so the smell drives plague away,
Place chicken bottoms on your spots and then you'll be OK.

CHORUS

First you feel a little poorly, then you start to swell

Then you start to spit some blood, and then you really smell

Then you know it's time to ring your fu-ne-ral bell

Then along comes Mister Death and swishes you to ... well!

The plague kills little children even more than mums or dads.

A priest he said it's because the wicked kids have acted bad.

Half the people on the earth are simply blown away.

So for Mister Death these will be really busy days.

CHORUS

First you feel a little poorly, then you start to swell

Then you start to spit some blood, and then you really smell

Then you know it's time to ring your fu-ne-ral bell

Then along comes Mister Death and swishes you to ... well!

Lyrics by Terry Deary

PLAYS AND PIGEONS
THEATRE, PLAGUES AND CURES

1

LIFE FOR QUEEN LIZ WASN'T ALL ABOUT BEING CRUEL TO CATHOLICS AND COUSINS. SOMETIMES SHE LIKED TO GET AWAY FROM THE MURDER, THE HORROR AND THE BLOODSHED. QUEEN LIZ ENJOYED THE THEATRE WHERE, FOR A CHANGE, SHE COULD WATCH WONDERFUL PLAYS ... ABOUT MURDER, HORROR AND BLOODSHED. PLAYS BY CLEVER WRITERS LIKE WILLIAM SHAKESPEARE.

SHAKESPEARE LIVED IN VIOLENT TIMES, SO MANY OF HIS PLAYS WERE PRETTY VIOLENT TOO. TAKE 'TITUS ANDRONICUS'. A HORRIBLY HISTORICAL PLAY. IT WAS SET IN ROME AND STARTED WITH TITUS MAKING A HUMAN SACRIFICE - THE SON OF TAMORA.

> TAKE YOUNG ALARBUS TO THE ALTAR, CUT HIM INTO PIECES THEN BURN HIM AS A SACRIFICE TO MY DEAD SONS

> THAT'S NOT VERY FAIR, MUM!

> I TOLD HIM THAT, SON, BUT THE OLD FOOL WON'T LISTEN

BUT TITUS'S DAUGHTER, LAVINIA, IS THE REAL LOSER. SHE OVERHEARS A REVENGE PLOT TO KILL TITUS. THE PLOTTERS HAVE TO SILENCE HER...

> YOU CAN'T STOP HER, AARON

> OH YES I CAN!

> I'M GOING TO TELL, AND YOU CAN'T KILL ME COS I'M AN UNARMED WOMAN. TELL HIM, TAMORA

BUT WHEN TAMORA ARRIVES AT THE FEAST, TITUS GIVES HER SOME NASTY NEWS...

> YUMMY. TASTY PIE. SHAME ABOUT THE FINGERNAIL INSIDE IT.

> YES, TAMORA, YOU HAVE JUST EATEN YOUR SONS. I HAD THEM KILLED AND BAKED IN THE PIE

> NOW IT'S YOUR TURN, QUEEN TERRIBLE TAMORA!

> NOW IT'S YOUR TURN, OLD TWIT-HEAD TITUS!

> NOW IT'S YOUR TURN, SAVAGE SATURNINUS!

HIGH-SPEED HISTORY

WHERE THERE'S MISERY, THERE'S MONEY. GET YOUR PLAGUE CURES HERE! ONLY A SHILLING

HAS THE PLAGUE GIVEN YOU A BAD LIVER?

TAKE A PINT OF ALE

POP ON NINE LICE FROM YOUR HAIR

DRINK THIS EVERY MORNING FOR A WEEK

HAS THE PLAGUE GIVEN YOU SWOLLEN BITS UNDER YOUR ARMS?

BOIL A RED-HAIRED DOG IN OIL

STIR IN WORMS AND MARROW FROM PIG BONE

PLASTER IT ON THE SWOLLEN BIT

BUT RUNNING AWAY WAS THE ONLY REAL ANSWER...

TO FLEE OR NOT TO FLEE, THAT IS THE QUESTION

People died, but Liz the last Tudor lived on. The problem was she was too old and tired to rule the country. She wouldn't say who would rule once she was dead. The Queen had no children and had never married. But she liked young men. Maybe a young lord could marry her and, when she hopped the twig, England would have a strong young king.

Maybe...

4

DRESS LIKE A TERRIBLE TUDOR

TERRIBLE TUDOR TROUSERS

If you'd like to act like a Tudor, feel like a Tudor, or if you're off to a fancy-dress party, you may like to try making these Tudor "hose".

1 Wear a pair of tights or tight trousers first.
2 Take a pair of old, baggy trousers. Cut them off at the knee. Slit them as shown.
3 Put the baggy trousers on over the tights. Tie them at the knee with ribbon or a scarf.
4 Stuff the baggy trousers with material of a different colour so it shows through the slits.
5 Wear a loose shirt and ruff and a belt with a sword or dagger – wooden, of course.
6 Go around saying, 'To be or not to be', or 'Alas, poor Yorick'. (They're famous lines from William Shakespeare plays – adults and teachers will be totally impressed.)

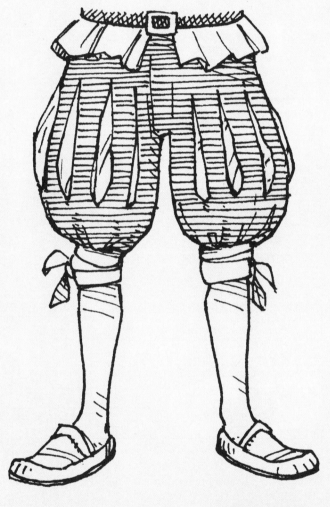

IT'S RUFF AT THE TOP!

A RUFF IDEA

1 Take seven 24-cm doilies (lacy paper table decorations, usually used at parties).

2 Cut them in half.

Use sticky tape to attach them to a 4-m strip of ribbon, allowing enough ribbon to tie at the back.

3 Make 2-cm folds in the doilies folding each one into a fan shape.

4 Keep the folds in place at the ribbon end with small stitches or sticky tape.

5 Tie the ends of the ribbon around your neck.

6 Wear with a collarless shirt (boys) and your terrible Tudor trousers.

Girls, wear with a blouse and full-length skirt.

7 Stroll around singing *Greensleeves*.

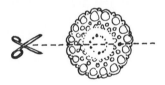

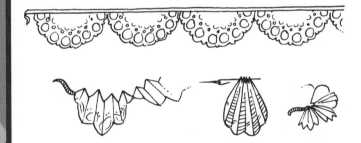

QUILL BILL

If you'd really like to know what it was like to write with a quill pen then you could try making one.

YOU NEED

• A strong feather – goose quill is best, but turkey or any other strong feather will do.

• A pen-knife – if you haven't a pen-knife then a Stanley knife will be just as good.

• Tweezers.

• Ink.

And an adult to make sure you don't get chopped fingers on the table!

HOW TO MAKE IT

1 Shorten the feather to about 20 cm.

2 Strip off all the barbs (the feathery part) from the shaft. (Yes, I know! In all the pictures you've seen the writers appear to be writing with feathers. They hardly ever did they only used the shaft and threw the rest away. Honest!)

3 Cut the bottom of the shaft off with your pen-knife (Figure 1).

4 Shape the bottom of the shaft as in Figure 2. Take out the core with tweezers.

5 Make a slit at the end of the nib about 5 mm long (Figure 3).

6 Trim the end of the shaft again, this time at an angle. (Figure 4 shows the angle for a right-handed writer)

7 Dip the quill in ink. Try writing an alphabet.

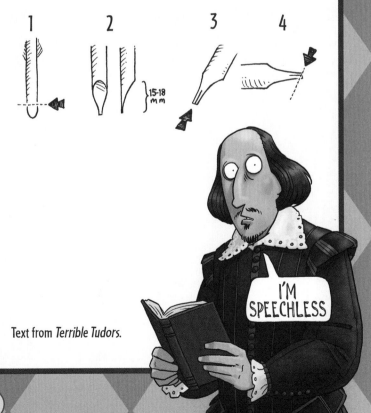

Text from *Terrible Tudors*.

TERRIBLE TUDOR PARTY

Why not have a putrid party and give your foul friends a feem ... I mean a theme. Why not a Shakespeare party? He has hundreds of cool characters you could dress as OR go along as a posh Tudor person ... maybe super Shakespeare or evil Elizabeth or her jolly executioner? Or a pathetic peasant perhaps? Wear your own home-made ruffs, but PLEASE do not go around and say to one another "You look a bit ruff today. Hah! Hah" because that is a very old, and very bad joke. Eat Tudor food and have a leather Tudor bucket for anyone who feels sick. Do NOT stretch anyone on a rack unless there is an adult present and if a Spanish Armada tries to invade your party call the Royal Navy. If an enemy cannonball heads your way call "Drake" and duck. (Which is rather a clever joke if you think about it? Oh, never mind.) Above all have as much fun as Anne Boleyn had in the Tower.

Tudor foods you may want to eat

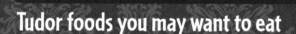

EGGS IN MUSTARD SAUCE

Ingredients :
Eggs- one for each person
& for each egg –
25 g butter
5 ml mustard (1 teaspoon)
5 ml vinegar (1 teaspoon)
A pinch of salt

Cooking :
Boil the eggs for 5 to 6 minutes.
While the eggs are boiling put the butter in a small saucepan and heat it.
When the butter has melted and begins to turn brown, take it off the heat.
Stir in the salt, mustard and vinegar.
When the eggs are ready remove the shells, cut them into quarters and put them on a warm dish.
Heat up the sauce again and pour it over the eggs.

ye womans weekly pg 77

ye olde New Idea

JUMBLES (KNOTTED BISCUITS)
Ingredients :
2 eggs   15 ml aniseed or caraway (3 teasp)
100 sugar   175 g plain flour
Cooking :
Beat the eggs. Add the sugar and aniseed (or caraway) and beat again. Stir in the flour to make a thick dough. Knead the dough on a floured board. Make the dough into rolls 1 cm wide by 10 cm long. Tie the strips into a single knot. Drop the knotted dough (6 at a time) into a pan of boiling water. They will sink to the bottom so use a spoon after a minute to help them float to the top. When the knots have floated for a minute and swelled, take them out of the water and let them drain on a wire rack. Put the knots on buttered baking sheets and bake for 15 minutes at Gas Mark 4 (or 350 degrees F. or 180 degrees C.). Turn them over and bake for another 10 minutes until they are golden brown.

page 106

DRAW YOUR OWN BEASTLY BUNTING

GROOVY GAMES WITH WICKED WORDS

People have always enjoyed playing word games. 'I spy with my little eye' is perfect for people with a great amount of time and a small amount of brain. But to really enjoy words you should try something a bit more challenging. Here are some wicked word games ...

KNICKERS

For: Two or more players.
Rules: Dead simple. One player must answer every question with a single word each time ... choose a word like 'slime', 'snot', 'eyeballs' or something equally disgusting. However, if they laugh (or even give a hint of a Mona Lisa smile) they have lost.

Here's an example where the answer word is knickers ...

Q: What do you wear on your head when you go to bed?
A: Knickers
Q: What do you call your cat?
A: Knickers
Q: What do you use to strain your tea?
A: Knickers

AMAZING ANAGRAMS

Mix up the letters of a word and spell a new word. That's an anagram. So t-a-m-e can become meat, mate or team.

Here are some clever anagrams you can bore your friends/family/teachers with. Say, 'Did you know...?

1 astronomer is an anagram of moon starer

2 schoolmaster is an anagram of the classroom

4 slot machines is an anagram of cash lost in 'em

7 punishment is an anagram of nine thumps

Got the idea? Then solve these anagrams (with the help of a clue) to give two famous names ...

Text from *Wicked Words.*

36

1 Hated for ill – he was hated because of what he did in the war!

2 Old west action – and he stars in films with plenty of that action.

Answers: 1 Adolf Hitler 2 Clint Eastwood

PANGRAMS

If you can't manage an anagram then try a pangram. What has this sentence got?

Six crazy kings vowed to abolish my quite pitiful jousts

It is a pangram because it has all 26 letters of the alphabet in it. There are 47 letters in that sentence. Can you create a pangram with fewer?

ODDBOD BOYS

Is your name an anagram? Here are some sentences that contain mixed-up boys' names. Can you **a)** find the boy's name then **b)** untangle it? (Are you one of them?)

1 Here comes Slime.
2 Evil's his name.
3 He should be Nailed.
4 Larches is very wooden.
5 Lace is very rich.
6 Every school needs a Warden.

DRAW YOUR OWN PIRATE FLAG

Everybody knows Pirates flew skull-and-cross-bone flags

But did you know that flags often had bleeding hearts or daggers or whole skeletons on them. Black Barty designed his own flag, showing a giant figure of himself standing, sword in hand, astride two skulls labelled ABH ('A Barbadian's Head') and AMH ('A Martinican's Head').

Calico Jack

Blackbeard

Black Barty

Henry Every

Thomas Tew

Stede Bonnet

NOW DRAW YOUR OWN PIRATE FLAGS. AARGH!

39

JOKE MACHINE

What did the Pharaoh say when he saw the pyramid?
Mummy's home.

Where did Caesar keep his armies?
Up his sleevies.

Why do mummies not tell secrets?
They keep everything under wraps.

What was the most popular film in ancient Greece?
Troy Story.

Why was King Alfred called 'the Great'?
Because Alfred the Blooming Marvellous would have sounded silly.

Why did the pupil miss his history exam?
He had the wrong date.

Where was Hadrian's Wall?
At the bottom of Hadrian's garden

Why did the Romans build straight roads?
So Britons couldn't hide round corners.

How did Vikings signal from ship to ship?
They used Norse code.

Where did the Vikings land when they came to England?
On their feet.

What's another term for Middle Ages?
Knight time.

How do you make a Mexican chilli?
Take him to the North Pole.

Why did Anne Boleyn not stand still when she was being executed?
She fancied a run round the block.

What did the executioner say to the prisoner?
Time to head off.

Why did the pirate need some soap?
To wash himself ashore.

What do pirates eat for tea?
Pieces of skate

Why is history the fruitiest subject at school?
It's full of dates.

What did the dragon say when he saw the knight in shining armour?
I hate tinned food.

What was Queen Vic short for?
So she could touch her toes.

HOW TO DRAW A GORGEOUS GEORGIAN

Martin Brown explains how to draw a Georgian lady.

YOU'LL NEED...
- A SHARP PENCIL ✓
- A RUBBER ✓
- AN INK PEN ✓
(if you want to colour the drawing)

1

Martin says: "I like to use reference books, but I probably can't make the dress as silly as they were in Georgian times. The dresses went out sideways – some of them were nine feet wide!"

2

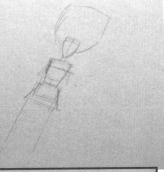

"I'll start with the simple box frame – even though she has a large dress on, her waist is still pulled in. A woman's hips are a bit wider."

3

"This time we have hair – lots of it! The hair is the point of the joke here, so let's have fun with it..."

4

"I'll put a slight angle on the hairdo, as if it's almost falling off."

5

"Make sure you are happy with the eyes when you are drawing. In a drawing like this everybody looks at the eyes first."

GRIM GHOSTS

Poor people couldn't afford to go to the theatre. So in the dim and flickering firelight of a gloomy evening, how did they entertain themselves? With stories.
And what better than a ghost story. Especially if it was a true ghost story. Here is a case from Cornwall about some villainous Victorians to chill your bones colder than a tombstone in the snow...

Listen, me dears, and I'll tell you the tale of two brothers. One brother was Edmund Norway and he was a seaman. On the night of 8th February 1840 he went to bed in his cabin and fell asleep around 11 p.m. He was a thousand miles away from his home in Cornwall.

He soon had a terrible dream that made him wake up sweating and screaming. He told it to the ship's officer, Henry Wren. He said...

'I dreamed I saw my brother killed. He was riding his horse along the road from Bodmin to Wadebridge. As he rode two men attacked him, and I watched in horror as one pointed a pistol at my brother. The pistol misfired twice so they dragged him from the horse and used the pistol to club him to death before they robbed him. Then one man dragged him across the road and dropped him in a ditch. I have a terrible fear that my brother has been murdered.'

Officer Wren said, 'It was just a bad dream. Go back to sleep. We'll be home in a week and you'll see your brother is safe and sound.'
But when Edmund Norway landed there was terrible news for him.
'Your brother, Nevell, has been murdered,' they said.

The constables had made an arrest. On 13th April William Lightfoot and his brother were found guilty of murdering Nevell Norway and sentenced to hang. Before he died, William confessed.

'I met my brother at the top of Dummer Hill and we plotted to rob the next person who came along. Around 11 p.m. we saw a man riding his horse along the road from Bodmin to Wadebridge. As he rode we two attacked him. He refused to hand over his money so I pointed my pistol at him. The pistol misfired twice so we dragged him from the horse and used the pistol to club him to death before we robbed him. Then my brother dragged him across the road and dropped him in a ditch.'

How did Edmund Norway know about his brother's death a thousand miles away and sailing in an ink-black sea?

Perhaps his brother's dying spirit slipped into his dreams to say farewell? Who knows? There's nothing as mysterious as death.

So, when the night time comes, and darkness falls, go gently, my dears, and may the angels watch over you.

Story from *Villainous Victorians*

DRESS UP TOMMY

1. THE TEDDY BEAR

Army jerkin made from goat-skin. It is given out in winter 1914 when the troops get cold – but not as cold as the goat that lost its skin.

2. THE BRITISH WARM

An overcoat, knee-length and tight at the waist. Cosy, but it's only for troops on horseback – and officers, of course.

3. NECKLET

A silk-lined collar which is supposed to stop a large, speeding bullet taking your head off.

4. THE BRODIE

A British steel helmet, invented in February 1916 for snipers – ace shooters who hide and take potshots at the enemy. Some officers have started to buy them for themselves. The shape is just like the ones worn by English archers at the Battle of Agincourt – and that was in 1415. John L Brodie invented the 1916 one.

5. BULLET-PROOF BIBLES

Pocket-sized copies of the New Testament have suddenly sold in tens of thousands. They are being bought by worried British mothers for their sons. There are stories of bullets being stopped by these little Bibles. There may be one or two true cases of Bibles stopping 'spent' rifle bullets. They are not a lot of good against high-explosive shells and machine-gun bullets. Still it's good to have God on your side – or your front.

Text and artwork taken from *Terrible Trenches* pages 10-11.

2

3

Make a slit along
the dotted line.

4

1

5

fold   fold

49

DRESS-UP TOMMY

(You might want an adult to help you with the fiddly bits.)

1 Cut this page out of the annual or make a colour photocopy if you don't want to damage it.

2 Roughly cut around Tommy and stick him on to a piece of thin card.

3 When the glue is dry, carefully cut around Tommy and fold the stand back where shown.

4 Cut around the clothes and fold the tabs to fix them on to Tommy.

5 Carefully cut a small slit in Tommy's helmet so it will fix on his head.

PUTRID PRIZES

If you want to win a host of *Horrible Histories* goodies, now's your chance. Draw your own vicious version of your favourite *Horrible Histories* character and send it to us at **HH Towers** at the address below.

There will be one first prize of *The Beastly Best Bits*, **Galt's Awesome** Art Set, Horrible Histories Top Trumps Turbo **game, a selection of Horrible Histories stationery and** Horrible Histories toys. **The ten runners-up will receive prizes of** *The Beastly Best Bits* **and a selection** of Horrible Histories stationery.

Don't forget to add your details to the back of the entry, so that we know where to send the prizes.
Have you written your ... name, age, address and postcode?
Please get your parent or guardian to sign the back of your entry before you put it into an envelope.

Send your entry to:
Horrible Histories Annual 2014 Competition
Scholastic Children's Books
Euston House
24 Eversholt Street
London
NW1 1DB

The competition closes on 14th April 2014, and winning entrants will be notified within one month of the closing date.

Savage small-print

Send entries to: Horrible Histories Annual 2014 Competition, Scholastic Children's Books, Euston House, 24 Eversholt Street, London, NW1 1DB. Entrants must be under 18 years old and must ask permission from a parent or guardian before entering. Entries are only valid if they include a drawing, your name and address. The first-prize winner and runners-up automatically accept that Scholastic Children's Books will be using their address to notify them of their prize. One entry per person only. All entries will be entered into the prize draw. The first-prize winner will be chosen by the judges after the closing date. The runners-up will be the next 10 entries selected by the judges. The judges' decision is final and no correspondence will be entered into. All entries shall become the property and copyright of Scholastic Ltd. This competition is open to all *Horrible Histories Annual 2014*, published by Scholastic Ltd, readers that are residents of the UK, Channel Islands and Isle of Man. The first-prize includes a selection of Horrible Histories gifts and books. The 10 runners-up prizes include a selection of Horrible Histories gifts and books. The names of the first-prize winner and runners-up may be shared with the companies and organizations with which the competition is being run for the purposes of prize delivery. Prizes are subject to availability. If in circumstances beyond our control we are unable to organize a prize, we will endeavour to organize an alternative prize of a similar value. No cash alternative will be offered. Entries must not be sent in through agents or third parties. Any such entries will be invalid. The first-prize winner and runners-up will be notified in writing within 28 days of the closing date. If an entry chosen to be a prize-winner does not include valid contact details or the prize-winner rejects the prize, Scholastic Ltd will draw a replacement prize-winner. Scholastic Ltd reserves the right to cancel the competition at any stage, if deemed necessary or if circumstances arise outside our control. Entrants will be deemed to have accepted these rules and agreed to be bound by them when entering a competition. No purchase is necessary. You can contact us in relation to this competition at Scholastic Children's Books, Euston House, 24 Eversholt Street, London, NW1 1DB. The competition closes at 12 midnight British Summer Time on 14th April 2014. No entries will be accepted after that date and no responsibility will be accepted for entries lost or damaged.

OUT OF TIME!

The 20th century was a great hundred years for inventions. Here are 14 important 20th-century things. But how many were first made in the last century?

ODD ONE OUT	RIGHT	WRONG		RIGHT	WRONG
1. Aeroplane	☐	☐	8. Getaway car	☐	☐
2. Cinema	☐	☐	9. Police car	☐	☐
3. Barbed wire	☐	☐	10. Chewing gum	☐	☐
4. Underground railway	☐	☐	11. Motor cars	☐	☐
5. Machine gun	☐	☐	12. Record player	☐	☐
6. Double glazing	☐	☐	13. Margarine	☐	☐
7. Flame-thrower	☐	☐	14. Teddy Bear	☐	☐

Answers on page 61.

Text from *The Massive Millennium Quiz Book*

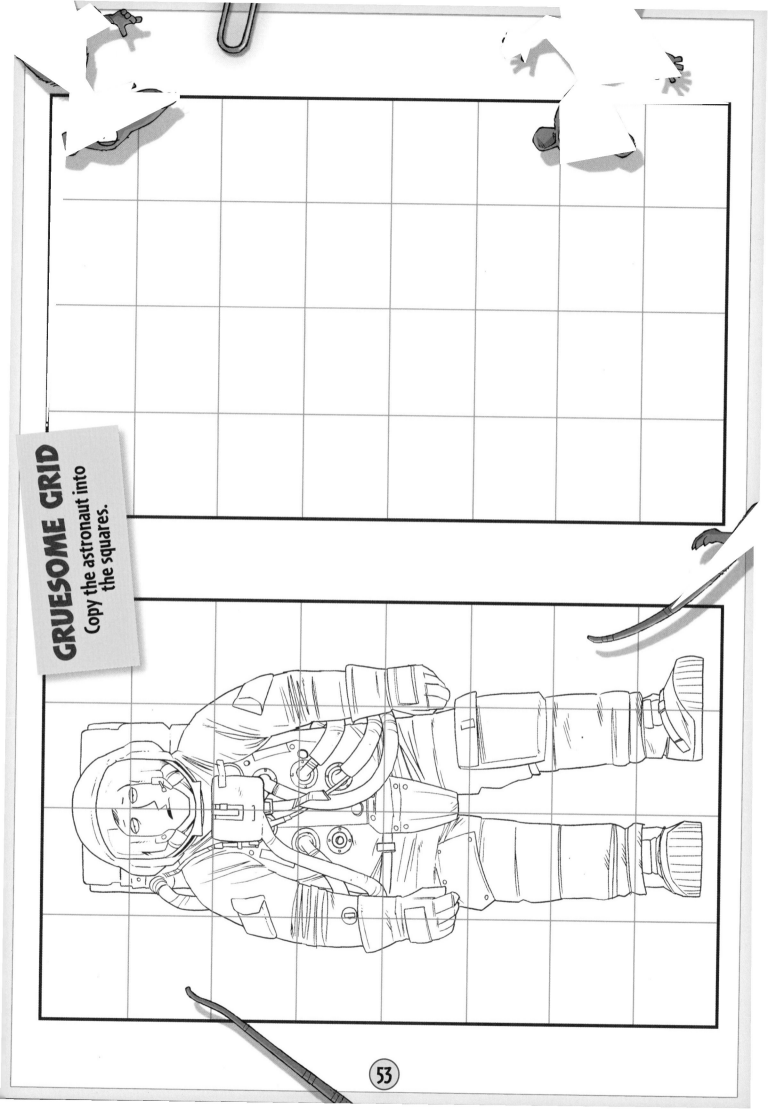

GRUESOME GRID
Copy the astronaut into the squares.

THE BIG QUIZ

1 Queen Elizabeth I was a measly monarch who ruled for 45 years between 1558 and 1603. Which of these foul facts is true?
a) She ate hedgehogs every day
b) She had the first flushing toilet in Britain
c) She made dogs lick her feet clean

2 In 1642, who did King Charles I and his Cavaliers begin to battle?

3 Who is this ruthless rebel, who tried to throw the English out of Scotland in 1297?
a) William Wallace
b) Bruce Banner
c) Frederick Forsyth

4 In Victorian times, villains began attacking victims using a horrible method of crushing their windpipe. What was this called?
a) Carroting
b) Vomiting
c) Garroting

5 TRUE or FALSE? In Georgian times, a cure for having a stye on your eyelid was to rub it with the tail of a black cat.

6 Attila the Hun was a fierce warrior who slaughtered thousands in Asia and Europe, but what caused his own death in ad 453?
a) Poison
b) Nose bleed
c) Belly ache

7 What did a Roman solider wear under his leather skirt?
a) Nothing
b) Underpants
c) Fig leaves

8 In 1588 England came under attack from Spain's navy. What were their fleet of ships known as?

9 Answer 'WWI' or 'WWII' to these five statements, depending on if you think they happened in the First World War or the Second World War...
• Germany invades Poland and shares it with the Soviets.

GOOD LUCK

- Poison gas is first used against soldiers in the trenches.
- Enemies stop fighting for a day or two and play friendly football matches.
- The Royal Air Force is formed and goes into battle.
- The Home Guard is established to protect Britain from enemy invasions.

10 Which two of Henry VIII's wives had their heads chopped off?

Catherine of Aragon

Anne Boleyn

Jane Seymour

Anne of Cleves

Kathryn Howard

Katherine Parr

11 After evil Oliver Cromwell died in 1658, which king had his body dug up, cut up, thrown in the Thames and stuck his head on a pole for a) 25 years?

b) Richard I

c) Charles II

d) Dave III

12 Unscramble these words to reveal what caused the English Peasants' Revolt in 1381. (Clue: it's very 'taxing'!)

LAX PLOT

13 What tax did Elizabeth I introduce that only men could pay?

14 Can you name these two Roman leaders?

JULIUS _____

MARK _____

15 Fill in the missing word from these three ruthless rulers!

WILLIAM THE

HARALD THE

VLAD THE

16 Which one of these was NOT a real food from the measly Middle Ages...

a) Mashed deer tongues

b) Pickled puffin

c) Roast peacock

d) Yorkshire pudding

17 Can you name this horrible villain?
I helped overthrow the king of France
I wanted to invade Britain but Lord Nelson put a stop to that!

18 Which people worshipped which god.
GREEKS. VIKINGS. INCAS. EGYPTIANS. ROMANS.
a) ANUBIS, God of the dead
b) THOR, God of thunder
c) VIRACOCHA, Creator of the Earth
d) POSEIDON, God of the sea
e) MARS, God of war

19 Where do some historians believe British warrior leader Boudica is buried?
a) Under London Bridge
b) Next to Hadrian's Wall, but on the Scottish side
c) Under Platform 8 of King's Cross station

20 Which of these was a Norman game?
a) Conkers
b) Chess
c) Pokémon

21 When he was a prince escaping from England (because his dad had lost the Civil War), James II dressed as:
a) A girl
b) A servant
c) Little Red Riding Hood

22 Which animals did doctors at the time think spread the plague in London in 1665?

23 What was the name of the person on board a pirate ship whose job it was to keep the gunners supplied with gunpowder?
a) Gun Weasel
b) Powder Monkey
c) Water Giraffe

24 TRUE or FALSE? Pirates often made their enemies walk the plank.

25 TRUE or FALSE? Roman gladiators fought these animals in the arena.
a) Lion   b) Turkey   c) Bear
d) Rabbit   e) Deer

26 The Spanish had a nickname for Francis Drake, 'El Draco'. What does that mean?

a) The dragon

b) The duck

c) The red-beard

27 Which Roman emperor did Cleopatra have a son with in 47 BC?

28 What did Tom McCarty use to hold up a bank in Denver, USA in 1889?

a) A strongly worded letter

b) A picture of a gun

c) A bottle of water

29 Which of these was a Victorian name for a policeman?

a) Raw lobster

b) Pickled egg

c) Sliced ham

30 Which of these plants did Celts (ancient tribes that lived in England) think were magical?

Mistletoe

Palm tree

Christmas tree

31 TRUE or FALSE? Open sewers ran through the streets in some Tudor towns.

32 What stopped George I from going to the funeral of his wife Dorothea, who he hated?

a) He got lost

b) He died

c) He needed the loo

33 What did Vikings make their soap from?

a) Flour

b) Conkers

c) Beer

34 Henry VIII wanted to make an example of rebels in 1537. Where did he have them hanged?

a) In the Tower of London so the whole city could see them.

b) In their gardens so their families could see them.

c) From the masts of ships so they could tour the country and be seen in every port.

NO TALKING

THE BIG QUIZ

35 Which giant statue in Egypt has the legs of a lion and the face of a woman?

36 How did Napoleon lose 380,000 men when he attacked Russia in 1812?
a) The Russian Army destroyed the French with cannons
b) The Russians poisoned the French
c) The Russians lost to the French

37 What was the Norman punishment for murder?
a) Hanging by the neck till dead
b) Having your eyes gouged out
c) Beheading (with a blunt axe)

38 Which of these was a food eaten by Viking warriors?
a) Ostrich
b) Guinea pig
c) Polar bear

39 TRUE or FALSE. Unmarried Elizabethan girls would wear a special hat in public.

40 Which of these was a cure for ringworm in the Middle Ages?
a) Washing your hair in a boy's pee
b) Wearing a dried toad around your neck
c) Breathing in the smoke of burned feathers

41 Where did someone called a "tosher" find money in Victorian times?
a) In freshly dug graves
b) Other people's pockets
c) Down toilets, in sewers and in drains.

42 TRUE or FALSE
a) Romans ate stuffed dormice!
b) In the First World War the German soldiers often kept cats as pets to deal with all the rats.
c) There were usually more sailors than rats on a pirate ship.

43 TRUE or FALSE Some ancient Greeks sacrificed vegetables instead of animals to the gods.

44 What was Oliver Cromwell given in 1657 that had never been seen in England before?
a) A pineapple
b) A banana
c) A mince pie

45 What did the Saxons sometimes use to make soap powder?
a) Bogeys
b) Spit
c) Pee

46 What did teachers at St Paul's School collect in the Middle Ages?
a) Stamps
b) Pee
c) Poo

47 What did sailors in Nelson's navy do with the hard cheese they were given to eat?
a) Used it as ammunition
b) Used it to catch mice
c) Made buttons out of it

48 Ancient Romans used a special sauce on their food made from:
a) Sheep's eyes
b) Fish guts
c) Monkey brains

49 What would a British solider in the First World War call "Dog and Maggot"?
a) Rifle and bullets
b) Socks and shoes
c) Bread and cheese

50 In the American Civil war, what did the Rebels sometimes use to make gunpowder when they ran low on supplies?
a) Buffalo poo
b) Human wee
c) Frog guts

Quiz questions taken from Horrible Histories Magazine Issue 6.

PENS DOWN

AWESOME ANSWERS

Where's Ratty? Page 16

Out of time! page 22

1 Soap factory – Right. In Sopars Lane London, 1259.

2 Hand gun – Wrong. First reported in 1338.

3 Glass factory – Right. First set up in Chiddingfold, Surrey, in 1229.

4 Water pipes – Right. Water was piped in Paddington in 1233.

5 Guillotine – Wrong. First reported in Ireland in 1307, but it wasn't known as a 'guillotine' until the French Revolution.

6 Windmill – Right. Common in Norfolk in the 1260s.

7 Clock – Right. First made in Britain at Dunstable Priory in 1283.

8 Vicar – Right. First seen in Gloucestershire, 1205.

9 Elephant – Right. Given as a gift to King Henry in 1256.

10 Knitting – Wrong. Norfolk 1533.

11 Spectacles – Right. Invented around 1287 in Italy.

12 Hymn book – Wrong. 1501.

13 Sack of sugar – Right. Moroccan sugar on sale in Durham 1299.

14 Glass mirror – Right. Described by a monk in 1279.

15 Cabbage – Wrong. 1531.

16 Pillory – Right. Wallingford 1231.

Warring Women Page 24

a) IRON LEG
b) ARMIES
c) SKELETONS
d) BABY
e) ADJUSTABLE ARMOUR
f) WILD ANIMALS
g) BOYFRIEND
h) VIKINGS

Spot the Lot! Page 46

Out of time! page 52

1 Aeroplane – Yes. First powered heavier-than-air flight in USA, 1903.
2 Cinema – No. New Orleans 1896.
3 Barbed wire – No. 1867
4 Underground railway – No. 1870.
5 Machine gun – No. First used in war in 1879.
6 Double glazing – No. England, 1874.
7 Flame-thrower – Yes. Gas-powered machine invented in Berlin, 1900.
8 Getaway car – Yes. Three Paris shop-robbers used one in 1901.

9 Police car – Yes. USA, 1903. (Two years after the first criminals used a car! A bit late!)
10 Chewing gum – No. 1872.
11 Motor cars – No. First petrol car 1883
12 Record player – No. 1879.
13 Margarine – No. 1869.
14 Teddy Bear – Yes. 1902 but the USA and Germany still argue over who had the first teddy.

THE BIG QUIZ page 54

1 b) She had the first flushing toilet. You could call that her royal throne!

2 Roundheads.

3 a) William Wallace. Don't call him a wally.

4 c) Garroting. No carrots were harmed.

5 True, but don't try this – it's not a good eye-dea!

6 Nose bleed. His nose started to bleed and he choked to death on his own blood. Lovely end to a lovely guy!

7 Underpants. What did you expect?

8 The Spanish Armada.

9 WWII. WWI. WWI. WWI. WWII.

10 Anne Boleyn and Kathryn Howard. Don't lose your head if you didn't get this one right!

11 b) Charles II. Olly was pretty smelly by then!

12 POLL TAX.

13 A Beard Tax. The bare-faced cheek!

14 Caesar & Antony.

15 CONQUEROR. RUTHLESS. IMPALER.

16 d) Yorkshire Pudding. The rest were all "delicacies" in the Middle Ages.

17 Napoleon Bonaparte.

18 a) Egyptians. b) Vikings. c) Incas. d) Greeks. e) Romans.

19 c) Under King's Cross Station. She's stuck because she doesn't have a ticket!

20 a) Conkers. We don't know if it was brought over by William the Conker-or!

21 a) A girl. He changed back or we'd have had Queen Jemima of England.

22 One point for any of dogs, cats, pigs, rabbits or pigeons. You can only get one point in total for this question though!

23 b) Powder monkey. It was normally a boy aged 11 or 12 – too young to fight with swords and pistols.

24 False! It was quicker just to chop their enemies to pieces!

25 a) True. b) False. Turkeys weren't introduced to Europe until the 1500s. c) True. d) False. e) True.

26 a) The Dragon. Drake was a monster to the Spanish!

27 Julius Caesar. Their son was called Caesarion.

28 c) A bottle of water. McCarty told the bank tellers that the bottle was full high explosives, but when he left he dropped the bottle in the bin. It was full of water!

29 a) Raw Lobster. Not because there was something fishy about them, but because a raw lobster is blue and so is a policeman's uniform.

30 Mistletoe. BUT it was only magical when it was cut by a druid using a gold sickle.

31 True. People often just emptied their chamber pots out of their windows!

32 b) He died on the way to the funeral.

33 b) Conkers.

34 b) He hung them in their gardens. What a horrible Henry!

35 The Sphinx.

36 c) The Russian Army were beaten by the French and retreated. The French followed them and were stuck in the middle of a deadly Russian winter.

37 b) The Normans rarely gave the death sentence to criminals, a murderer would normally lose his hands or eyes.

38 c) Polar bear.

39 False! They would show they were unmarried by not wearing ANY hat in public.

40 a) Pee! Burned feathers were a cure for fainting and the dried toad was a cure for bleeding inside the body.

41 c) In sewers and drains. Hopefully they were filthy rich.

42 True. They would be kept in the kitchen and fattened up with all the best food before being killed and stuffed. True. False. The crew of a Spanish ship once claimed to have killed 4,000 rats on one journey!

43 True.

44 a) A pineapple. Maybe as he was quite prickly!

45 c) Pee. They smelled wee-ly bad!

46 c) Pee. It was used to cure leather. Urgh!

47 c) They made buttons. Even the mice wouldn't eat the tough cheese.

48 c) Fish guts. They were soaked in salt water and left in the sun for a few days first. Blurgh!

49 c) Bread and Cheese.

50 b) The Rebels would dig up toilets to find potassium nitrate (saltpetre) that was an essential ingredient for gunpowder.